MY BEST FRIEND IS A DOLPHIN!

And More True Dolphin Stories!

Moira Rose Donohue

NATIONAL GEOGRAPHIC

WASHINGTON, D.C.

Since 1888, the National Geographic Society has funded more than 12,000 research, exploration, and preservation projects around the world. The Society receives funds from National Geographic Partners, LLC, funded in part by your purchase. A portion of the proceeds from this book supports this vital work. To learn more, visit natgeo.com/info.

NATIONAL GEOGRAPHIC and Yellow Border Design are trademarks of the National Geographic Society, used under license.

For more information, visit nationalgeographic.com, call 1-800-647-5463, or write to the following address:

National Geographic Partners
1145 17th Street N.W.
Washington, D.C. 20036-4688 U.S.A.

Visit us online at
nationalgeographic.com/books

For librarians and teachers:
ngchildrensbooks.org

More for kids from National Geographic:
kids.nationalgeographic.com

For information about special discounts for bulk purchases, please contact National Geographic Books Special Sales:
specialsales@natgeo.com

For rights or permissions inquiries, please contact National Geographic Books Subsidiary Rights: bookrights@natgeo.com

Designed by Ruth Ann Thompson

National Geographic supports K–12 educators with ELA Common Core Resources. Visit natgeoed.org/commoncore for more information.

Library of Congress Cataloging-in-Publication Data

Names: Donohue, Moira Rose, author.
Title: My best friend is a dolphin! / by Moira Rose Donohue.
Description: Washington, D.C. : National Geographic Kids, [2017] | Series: National geographic kids chapters | Audience: Ages 7-10. | Audience: Grades 4 to 6.
Identifiers: LCCN 2017010720 (print) | LCCN 2017029183 (ebook) | ISBN 9781426329043 (e-book) | ISBN 9781426329029 (pbk. : alk. paper) | ISBN 9781426329036 (hardcover : alk. paper)
Subjects: LCSH: Dolphins--Juvenile literature.
Classification: LCC QL737.C432 (ebook) | LCC QL737.C432 D665 2017 (print) | DDC 599.53--dc23
LC record available at https://lccn.loc.gov/2017010720

Printed in China
17/RRDS/1

Table of CONTENTS

A FISHY TALE: Kelly and the Katrina Eight   4

Chapter 1: Just Whistle   6

Chapter 2: Take the Bait   16

Chapter 3: The Katrina Eight   26

MY BEST FRIEND IS A DOLPHIN: Dean and JoJo   36

Chapter 1: Boy Meets Dolphin   38

Chapter 2: You're My Best Friend   48

Chapter 3: A Whale of a Tale   58

DOLPHINS TAKE CHARGE: Flip Nicklin, Photographer   68

Chapter 1: Revolving Romeo   70

Chapter 2: Photo Finish   80

Chapter 3: The Return of Echo and Misha   90

DON'T MISS!   99

Index and More Information   110

Jumping for joy! The rescuers and the missing dolphins are reunited!

A FISHY TALE:
Kelly and the Katrina Eight

A playful dolphin dances with a hula hoop.

Have you ever been outsmarted by a dolphin? Tim Hoffland has. The clever dolphin who tricked him is named Kelly. Tim didn't really mind being tricked. It just proved what he already knew: Dolphins are super smart! From the first time Tim saw a real dolphin, he knew that he wanted dolphins to be a part of his life.

Tim went to college in Wisconsin, U.S.A. During spring break one year, he went to an oceanarium (sounds like oh-shun-AIR-ee-um). That's an aquarium with marine mammals. Marine mammals are animals that live in the water but breathe air—like whales or dolphins.

Tim watched the dolphin show there. He stared in amazement as the dolphins flipped and tumbled. With just a hand signal from their trainers, they walked on their tails. *They're really smart!* he thought. After each trick, the dolphins swam up to their trainers. They opened their mouths for a tasty fish treat. They looked like they were smiling. Tim really was smiling. He was in love. And he knew what he was going to do after college. He would get a job as a marine mammal trainer.

After Tim graduated, he searched the country for places that worked with cetaceans (sounds like sih-TAY-shunz). That's what whales, porpoises, and dolphins are called. Millions of years ago, the ancestors of these animals had legs. They walked on land. But over time, they moved into the water to find new sources of food. There are two main types of cetaceans: toothed whales and baleen whales. Dolphins have teeth. So they are a type of toothed whale.

Tim applied for jobs wherever there were dolphins. Months went by. He was ready to give up. Then he got a call. The Institute for

Marine Mammal Studies (IMMS) wanted him to fly down for an interview. It's in Gulfport, Mississippi, U.S.A. Gulfport sits right on the Gulf of Mexico.

Tim was so nervous. He had looked for a job for a long time. This might be his only chance to work with dolphins. After he arrived, he met with one of the trainers. The trainer handed Tim a pair of rubber boots and coveralls. Then he told Tim to help unload a truck. The truck was filled with fish—49,000 of them! *This is not my idea of a job interview,* Tim thought. But he did it anyway. After all, he really wanted the job!

After he finished, he saw the dolphin tank. He stood looking at the animals. All at once, a dolphin popped up to the surface. She tossed him a hula hoop.

He didn't know what to do with it, so he flipped it back. She retrieved it! He looked into her eyes. *She understands,* he thought.

Tim got the job. He would help take care of dolphins and other animals. That meant unloading a lot of fish. It also meant learning a lot about dolphins. Tim learned about a dolphin's body. The snout is called the rostrum (sounds like RAHS-truhm). The fluke (sounds like FLOOK) is the tail. There's an opening on the back of a dolphin's head. It's called the blowhole. It's like a nostril. Dolphins breathe through it.

Tim also studied the way the dolphins acted. They loved to play. They turned almost anything that floated into a toy. Sometimes, they acted like clowns. They decorated themselves in seaweed.

From the beginning, Tim worked with trained dolphins in the dolphin shows. But he wanted to learn something more. He wanted to know *how* to train the dolphins to do new things. One day, a new trainer named Mike Magaw arrived. Mike gave Tim books to read. And Mike let Tim watch him train the dolphins. Tim saw that dolphins are not trained with words, like dogs are. They are trained to follow hand signals. And, of course, they don't get dog biscuits for a good job. They get fish!

Before long, Tim was helping Mike train the dolphins. Tim could see that the dolphins were enjoying the new tricks. They had a sparkle in their eyes. Tim understood that animals as smart as dolphins need to keep their minds active.

Dolphins vs. Porpoises

Dolphins and porpoises are both whales. In fact, they are both toothed whales. But dolphins are not the same as porpoises. They are more like cousins. Dolphins have long snouts. Porpoises have smaller, rounded rostrums. Picture a pug dog in your mind. Now think of a sleek greyhound. The smushed-face pug is like the porpoise. Most dolphins are bigger than porpoises. The biggest difference between these animals is their teeth. Porpoises have rounded teeth. Dolphins have pointy chompers.

Tim also saw that the dolphins had different personalities. One young dolphin named Jacki was very sweet. She was Tim's favorite. She was about the same age as another female named Kelly. Kelly was very smart. She learned new behaviors faster than any of the other dolphins.

Tim wanted to teach some of the dolphins to swim around the pool slapping their tails. That's a hard trick. To teach dolphins tricks that use several behaviors, trainers use a whistle. For this trick, Tim gave each dolphin the hand signal to flap her fluke in place. When she did it, he blew the whistle. Then he tossed the dolphin a fish. After a while, he only blew the whistle. That meant *Good job!* It also told the animal that she had to do something

Did You Know?

Dolphins can use tools. Some dolphins carry sponges in their mouths. They use them to protect their sensitive noses when they forage for food on the ocean floor.

more to get the treat. Tim held a target pole a short distance away. When the dolphin touched it with her rostrum, Tim blew the whistle again. Little by little, each dolphin swam around the tank, slapping her tail and touching the pole. Now it was time for a juicy fish!

Tim also taught the dolphins certain behaviors for their safety. One thing he wanted was to get their attention fast. For this behavior, Tim used a double whistle. It meant that the dolphins should stop what they were doing and come straight to the trainer. Tim didn't know it at the time, but this training would help save their lives one day.

Tim trains the dolphins to retrieve anything they find.

Chapter 2

TAKE THE BAIT

The dolphins already knew how to retrieve (sounds like ree-TREEV) toys. Tim would toss out a ball or hoop. Then he would bend his arm at the elbow, his fingers pointing up. With his palm facing the dolphin, he would push it down, toward the animal. It was the signal to retrieve. The dolphins would bring back whatever toys they found.

The dolphins were so good at retrieving, Tim decided to put this training to practical use. Visitors often dropped things into the dolphin tank by accident. *Oops, those were my favorite sunglasses!* Dolphins love to make toys out of anything new. But cameras and hats don't belong in their tank. Tim decided to teach the dolphins to fetch anything that didn't belong there.

Soon, when Tim gave the retrieve command, a dolphin would sometimes find a toy. But if a dolphin brought back a lost item, she got an extra big fish. Before long, the dolphins figured out that they would get big treats if they found lost items.

Kelly seemed to find items more quickly than the other dolphins. Tim would give the signal, and she would dive straight down.

Did You Know?

Different types of wild dolphins eat different types of fish. Some types like salmon, and some chow down on squid. But even though dolphins have teeth, they don't chew their food! They just swallow it whole.

Moments later, she would pop up again. She had something in her mouth every time. Sometimes it was just a small piece of trash. Other times it was a valuable lost item. Tim thought she was very smart. He would soon find out just how smart she really was.

Some scientists think dolphins are the second smartest animals on Earth. And they have a superpower, too. Dolphins use echolocation (sounds like ek-oh-loh-KAY-shun) to find things. That means they send out a stream of sounds underwater. *Click, click, click!* The sound bounces back to them. The sound waves form a picture in their minds. From that mental picture, dolphins can tell the size and shape of something. The echo also tells them how close something is. This super talent tells them if danger is nearby. It also helps them find food—or lost items!

The tank where Kelly and the other dolphins swam had windows on the lower level. People could watch the dolphins underwater. The dolphins would flip, twist, and kick. Sometimes they would come up to the windows. They would look at the visitors. One day, Tim was walking by a window. Kelly was floating in front of the window. Tim hadn't given the retrieve command, but Kelly had a piece of trash in her mouth. As soon as Tim noticed, she turned and splashed up to the surface. Kelly gave him the trash. Tim gave her a fishy treat. He was impressed!

Kelly started waiting at the window for Tim more and more often. Each time, she had a piece of trash or a lost item. Tim wondered, *Why does she find so much more trash than the other dolphins?* Then he got his answer. One day, the pool was being cleaned. The dolphins were safe in another pool. Tim went into the dry pool. In a far corner was a pile of rocks. Tim looked around them. That's when he discovered Kelly's secret. Kelly picked up trash whenever she found it.

Mirror, Mirror

Experts used to think that only people and some apes could recognize themselves in mirrors. But Diana Reiss and another scientist did a study with bottlenose dolphins. They found out that dolphins recognize themselves in mirrors, too. And they do more than just look. They study how they look. The scientists put marks on the dolphins. The dolphins swam straight to the mirror. They turned to see the mark better. But unlike chimps, the dolphins didn't look at marks on each other.

Then Kelly hid it. She had her own private trash stash! Whenever she wanted a treat, Kelly pulled something out. She waited at the window until she caught Tim's eye. As soon as he took the bait, she swam to the dock where the fish were kept. Tim laughed. *She's being lazy!* he thought. But she was also being a smarty-pants. She had figured this out all by herself. And she had outsmarted Tim!

Today, scientists are trying to test dolphins' intelligence (sounds like in-TELL-i-jens). They have created an experiment called the ELVIS project. The scientists show shapes on an underwater screen. Each shape represents a type of fish. The dolphin must aim its echolocation at the symbol. When it does, the dolphin gets that kind of treat. A dolphin named Luna was the first to learn how to find the right symbol to ask for her favorite.

Experiments like this tell us that dolphins are smart and fast learners. Tim knew that, too. And after Kelly's tricks, he wanted to know just *how* smart she was. Tim decided to try a different kind of test. He wanted to compare three dolphins. But it's hard to find ways to test dolphin smarts. So Tim met with another dolphin expert. Together, they designed a test.

First, they made a special plastic screen. The screen was clear, so the dolphins could see through it. Using a target pole, they taught three dolphins to swim to the screen. Then a trainer dove on the other side of the screen. He gave hand signals for behaviors the animals knew. The trainer would signal for a spin or a wave. Once the animals showed they knew the behaviors, it was time to darken the screen. That made it harder for them to see the signal. Eventually, Tim made the screen completely dark. Now the dolphins couldn't see the diver with their eyes. They had to use echolocation to "see" his signal. Pretty soon, they understood. Next, Tim used a computer to give him signals in a random order. He told the trainer who was hidden behind the screen what signal to give. The dolphins had to read the diver's signal and perform the right action. All three passed the test. One dolphin got it correct more than 90 percent of the time. It was Kelly, of course!

IMMS dolphins take over a hotel swimming pool during Hurricane Katrina.

Chapter 3

THE KATRINA EIGHT

Tim worked with his brainy student for many years. But Kelly's biggest test was still ahead. In 2005, a hurricane was headed for the United States. It was named Katrina (sounds like kuh-TREE-nuh). Hurricanes are superstorms. Moisture swirls into the air. Rain and wind pound the ground. Giant waves crash onto beaches. Streets flood. Buildings fall.

Gulfport was right in Katrina's path. On August 28, winds from Katrina were already blowing things around at the IMMS. Trash cans rattled and fell over. Trees swayed and bent. The full hurricane would arrive the next day. People were told to leave the shore area. But the staff had to protect the animals first. The director was desperate to find safe places for the dolphins. He called hotels that were inland. He asked if he could put some of the dolphins in their swimming pools. Two hotels agreed. The hotels were about four miles (6.4 km) away from the shore. *The dolphins should be safe here*, Tim thought.

Tim and the other trainers dropped canvas slings into the dolphin tank. They scooped out six of the dolphins.

Then they loaded them into trucks. The trainers climbed into the trucks, too. They sponged the dolphins with cold water. When the trainers unloaded the dolphins, the hotel guests stood outside. They watched as the dolphins were placed in the swimming pools. It was pretty strange.

Six dolphins were protected now, but that still left eight dolphins, including Kelly. The director told Tim that he thought they could stay at the IMMS. They would remain in the large steel tank. It had survived Hurricane Camille (sounds like kuh-MEEL) years earlier.

Tim checked on the dolphins. They didn't seem worried. Kelly and Jacki blew bubbles and played with toys. So, he said goodbye. Tim went to his home, 10 miles

(16 km) away, pulling several crated sea lions in a trailer.

The next morning, Katrina tore through the area. It caused a lot of damage. The towns on the coast were flooded. Huge trees toppled. Buildings were destroyed. About 2,000 people died. Others lost their homes. It was one of the worst hurricanes ever to hit the United States.

As soon as the winds died down, Tim drove to the IMMS to check on the dolphins. Tim felt uneasy, but he was not prepared for what they found. A 40-foot (12-m) wave had hit the dolphin tank. It had overflowed. The dolphins were gone!

Did You Know?

The center of a hurricane is called the eye. It's very calm. But the winds around it are usually the strongest.

The sea lions were missing, too. They had been carried into the streets of Gulfport. Sea lions can't live for long outside water. Tim and the other staff had to find them first. Some were 25 miles (40 km) away! When they found a sea lion, the workers put it into a wooden crate. They took the animals to new homes at different zoos in the region.

As soon as they had rounded up the sea lions, Tim was anxious to look for the eight dolphins. Had they been swept out to sea? The dolphin tank sat right on the shore. But the dolphins had lived at the center for a long time. They didn't know how to find food in the open water. Tim thought that the eight dolphins might not be able to live alone longer than a week.

Emergency workers were in the area. They told the trainers not to go into the water. It wasn't safe yet. Days went by. Tim was getting more and more worried. After 11 days, he and the other trainers were finally allowed to look for the animals. The local sheriff loaned them a helicopter to search from the air. And they went out in small boats. Tim and the other trainers went out on the boats. They banged things together to make noise. Then they used the special double whistle. *Ooweeeeee, ooweeeee!*

Suddenly, a dolphin head popped up. Then another. And another. The dolphins had heard the whistle. They were responding to their training!

Free Flipper

People love dolphin shows. Dolphins are so clever and playful. But some folks think it's not fair to use dolphins as entertainment. And others just want them to be free. Not long ago, the National Aquarium in Baltimore, Maryland, U.S.A., made a big decision. It would free its eight dolphins. Some other aquariums are thinking about doing the same. But it will take time to find the right place for the animals. The dolphins were raised in aquariums. They can't live on their own. They don't know how to catch their dinner. The National Aquarium is considering making a "sea pen" in the Caribbean or near Florida, U.S.A., for them to live in.

Tim counted. All eight dolphins were together! And they were less than a mile (1.6 km) from shore. Tim was overjoyed. But the dolphins were in bad shape. Some were covered in scratches and needed medicine. All the dolphins needed food. The trainers checked each dolphin carefully.

Next, they had to figure out how to rescue the dolphins. They decided to use large mats to carry them back to shore. The U.S. Navy brought in pools to hold the dolphins. Jacki and her daughter needed help and medicine first. Then Tim and the others took Kelly and one of the calves. But when the trainers went back, the last four dolphins had vanished!

Tim was shocked. *Where were they?* He thought about Kelly, who had been swimming on the edge of the group. She must have been keeping the dolphins together so that they could be found. Kelly was a natural leader and the most experienced. That's why the other dolphins followed. But once she was rescued, no one was left in charge. Without Kelly, the others had probably swam out to sea.

Tim and the other trainers searched farther out in the gulf. They finally found the other dolphins. All eight dolphins survived. They became known as the Katrina Eight. It was a remarkable rescue.

Kelly and the other Katrina Eight dolphins are retired now. They live in luxury, welcoming tourists to the sunny Bahama Islands.

JoJo shows Dean an underwater "treasure."

MY BEST FRIEND IS A DOLPHIN: DEAN and JOJO

Dean and JoJo glide side by side.

Chapter 1

BOY MEETS DOLPHIN

Most people have a best friend. It's the friend you spend all of your time with. It's the person you tell your secrets to. It's the one you trust most. Dean Bernal (sounds like ber-NAHL) has a best friend. His name is JoJo. But Dean's best friend is a little different. Dean's best friend is a dolphin!

Dean was about five years old when he came nose to rostrum with a dolphin. He and his family were at the beach in Santa Cruz, California, U.S.A. The surf was a little rough. A wave surprised Dean from behind. It knocked him over and tugged him under. Bubbles engulfed him. Dean opened his eyes under the water. Several dolphins surrounded him. One looked Dean in the eye—a look he would never forget. Dean suddenly felt calm. Then he felt something nudge him up to the surface. And someone yanked Dean out of the waves. He coughed and sputtered and spit out water. As soon as he could catch his breath, he tried to run back into the ocean. His mother stopped him.

"The dolphins!" he cried.

"There are no more dolphins," she said, looking around.

"Yeah," said young Dean. "They want to play."

But no one wanted Dean to go back in the water to look for them. After all, he had almost drowned. Years later, Dean met another dolphin. This time, Dean and the dolphin became best friends. And they still are.

Dean was on summer vacation from college. He was restless. He wanted to go somewhere by a beach, but he didn't know where. He stood in an airport in Florida, U.S.A., looking at flights. A stranger was standing next to him.

"You want to go here," she said. She pointed to a sign for Turks and Caicos (sounds like KAY-cohs). It's a chain of British islands in the Caribbean. On a whim, he bought a ticket.

Dean stayed in an area called Grace Bay. He loved the miles of white sand and crystal clear water. On his first day, he went swimming. He was exploring some reefs when he heard a chittering nearby. He looked around. And then he saw them.

There were three young bottlenose dolphins. They swam alongside him. Then one of them flipped around. Like the dolphin from long ago, this one looked Dean right in the eye. Dean felt a special connection to this dolphin. He decided to name him JoJo.

Dean met the dolphins again the next day. Two of them seemed more interested in playing with each other. But not JoJo. *Eeh-eeh-eeh-eeh,* he chattered. Then he flipped his tail. *Does he want me to follow?* Dean wondered. He swam after the dolphin. JoJo seemed to be giving him a tour. He pointed at animals in the reef. He stuck his rostrum into the sand and chased fish up. Then he clicked and looked at Dean as if to say, *Hey, did you see it?*

Dean swam every day. And JoJo swam with him. Dean didn't want to leave his new friend. He decided he would stay a little longer. So, he took a job as a scuba diving instructor.

How to "Squeak" Dolphin

Dolphins are chatty creatures. They chitter, chirp, and click. They even make a sound like a creaky door in a haunted house. *Squeeeeak!* They call each other with whistles. Before they are a year old, they pick a special whistle. They announce it to others as their name. Humans haven't been able to decode their language. But scientists in Hawaii, U.S.A., have taught dolphins a type of language that uses signs and sounds. It helps the humans and dolphins communicate. Scientists hope to decode dolphin language someday soon.

Dean started his classes in shallow water. He explained the diving equipment to his students. But soon after he started his class, JoJo barged in. He wanted Dean to come play with him. Dean couldn't leave the class, but JoJo didn't understand. He was like a pesky little brother. Dean tried to ignore him. JoJo poked the students with his rostrum. Finally, he swam off.

The next time Dean was teaching, JoJo glided in again. This time he tugged on Dean's rubber flippers. That made Dean flop headfirst into the water. Again Dean tried to ignore him.

When clowning around didn't work, JoJo brought friends to class. One day, he nudged a sea turtle right into the middle of the students. Show-and-tell, dolphin style!

Another time, he brought a more dangerous visitor—a very small shark. JoJo shoved the shark at the students. The shark swam in circles, stirring up the sandy floor. People panicked and started swimming in all directions. Class dismissed!

People at the diving school had a chat with Dean. JoJo was disrupting class too often. "Dean, you need to take your dolphin to the reef so we can continue our scuba lessons."

"Sure!" said Dean. He didn't mind getting paid to keep JoJo company!

Dean wanted to be able to see all the things that JoJo could show him. Dolphins can hold their breath for about 15 minutes. Dean worked really hard trying to hold his breath for longer and longer periods of time. Pretty soon,

Dean could lie on the bottom of the sea and blow bubbles. As they floated up, they grew bigger. They sparkled like diamonds. Sometimes JoJo would try to swim into them.

Dean and JoJo communicated mostly through body language. JoJo would point at things with his rostrum. Dean would point with his hand. JoJo knew to look where Dean pointed. Dolphins are one of the few animals that understand pointing. (Even chimpanzees don't get the point!) Dolphins use many different kinds of sounds to speak to each other. Dean didn't speak dolphin. But Dean noticed that JoJo used one sound over and over. *Weeee-hee-yoo.* One day, Dean figured it out. That whistle was JoJo's name for him.

JoJo and Dean, rostrum to nose!

Chapter 2

YOU'RE MY BEST FRIEND

People around the world heard about Dean and JoJo. And, of course, many of them wanted to meet these good buddies. Suddenly, visitors swarmed the islands. They trudged into the shallow waters hoping JoJo would swim by. Often, he did. The tourists sometimes tried to grab him or pet him. After all, who doesn't want to be close to a dolphin?

But wild dolphins don't like to be touched by human strangers. Even Dean didn't touch JoJo. To wild dolphins, a touch from a stranger is like a poke or a slap. Sometimes JoJo would slap them back with his tail or even bite. It wasn't long before JoJo got the reputation of being a troublemaker.

Dean heard rumors. Some people said that the local government was thinking about catching JoJo and moving him someplace else. Others said JoJo was going to be sent away to be trained. Dean was upset. He didn't want to lose his friend. And he wanted people to appreciate this beautiful wild creature. *How do you protect a wild dolphin?* Dean wondered.

Dean wrote letters to the local government and the tourist board. He even wrote to Prince Charles of Great Britain! He made statements to the public. He spoke to the government.

He told them that JoJo should be allowed to stay in his home. JoJo was a symbol of wildlife in this beautiful island country.

The Ministry of Natural Resources agreed to make a national park and marine preserve on the islands. It also announced that JoJo was a "national treasure." Dean was hired to protect JoJo. He became the official warden for the Queen of England's dolphin.

Dean took his job seriously. He wanted to know what to do if JoJo was injured. Helping a wild dolphin is different from

JO JO the DOLPHIN

helping a dolphin in captivity. Dolphins at oceanariums are trained to take medicines. Wild dolphins aren't. So Dean talked to cetacean (sounds like sih-TAY-shun) experts. He made a special first aid kit. Then he started the JoJo Project to teach people about wild dolphins. He also put up signs on the beach telling people not to touch JoJo.

JoJo was safer now. Tourists knew to leave him alone. But another danger threatened him. Visitors didn't just swim in the blue waters of the islands. They enjoyed other water sports. People rented speedboats, water skis, and water bikes.

Sometimes these watercraft raced so fast that dolphins couldn't get out of the way. The boats could seriously injure the animals. Dean convinced the government to limit the water bike area. But there was still one area near the beach where people could rent water bikes.

With his own money, Dean bought propeller guards. They were metal grates that fit over the propellers on boats. They would prevent the blades from cutting dolphins. The boat owners refused to use them. They said the guards would make the engines burn too much fuel.

One day, Dean was standing in the shallow water. A water biker turned sharply toward the shore. JoJo was right in his path. As Dean watched, the water bike raced ahead and hit the dolphin's back, hard. Blood swirled in the water. Dean ran out to JoJo.

JoJo was on his side. That meant his blowhole was underwater. He couldn't breathe.

Dean had never touched his friend before. In fact, he had told people many times, "Don't touch the dolphin; he'll bite!" But Dean knew he had to touch JoJo now. He had to rescue his friend. Dean put his arms around the dolphin's soft skin. He rolled JoJo right-side up. JoJo took a huge breath.

"Will he be all right?" someone called out. Dean wasn't sure. He could see a deep cut by JoJo's eye. Dean held him for a little while. JoJo didn't fight him. Then Dean let go. But JoJo shuddered and flipped over again. Dean rolled him upright again and again. Every time he let go, JoJo had another spasm (sounds like SPAZZ-um) and flipped over.

JoJo and his canine
friend, Toffee

All by Myself

Most dolphins live with other dolphins.
But not always. Now and then, a dolphin
is found living by itself. No one is sure why
this happens. It might be that the dolphin
has lost its parents. Or it might have been
pushed out of a pod, or group of dolphins.
Sometimes a dolphin chooses to live alone.
Solitary dolphins may look for human
friends. And sometimes, like people, they
pal around with dogs. A dolphin named
Duggie swam off the coast of an island
near Ireland. His best friend was Ben, a
dog. The two paddled together every day!

Dean didn't give up. It seemed like hours, but he kept turning JoJo over and holding him. JoJo trusted that his friend was trying to help him. Finally, JoJo kept his balance. He started to float away.

He'll probably go to the mangrove trees, Dean thought. It was a safe, quiet place with lots of shrubs to hide in. Dean started to follow him. But it was getting dark, and he knew he needed to get back to shore. The next morning, he went looking for his flippered friend. But JoJo was nowhere to be found. Dean was upset with himself. "I should have gone with him," he muttered. After all, JoJo was his best friend.

Days went by with no sign of JoJo. Dean was worried. He had trouble sleeping. After two weeks, Dean swam out to the reef.

"Hey, have you seen a dolphin?" he asked men on local fishing boats. They shook their heads. Finally, one man who didn't speak a lot of English said, "Dolphin. Yes!" He helped Dean onto his boat and took him to a shallow sandbar. *Chirp, chirp!* Dean heard. He jumped off the boat. He swam as fast as he could toward the sound. There was JoJo. He circled Dean. Dean could see that his cut was healing. Then JoJo looked Dean in the eye. Dean knew that JoJo wasn't mad at him for holding him. JoJo spun around and flipped his fluke. Dean knew what that meant. JoJo was saying, *Let's go exploring!*

Best friends Dean and JoJo explore the ocean floor.

Chapter 3

A WHALE OF A TALE

Dolphins love to play. JoJo and Dean liked to surprise each other. They played peekaboo and hide-and-seek. JoJo tried to imitate Dean with his flippers. Like other dolphins, JoJo loved to hide things. One time he took Dean to see something he had "found." It was a diver's camera. Dean is pretty sure that rascal took it and hid it from its owner!

JoJo took Dean to places that he wouldn't have discovered himself. Sometimes he would take Dean's hand in his mouth and guide him along. Other times Dean used a dive scooter. It has a small motor. Dean held it in both hands, and it pulled him along in the water. It helped him to swim faster, so he could keep up with JoJo.

Now and then, JoJo introduced Dean to other sea creatures. *Look!* JoJo would point with his rostrum. *A squid! Looks like lunch!* One sunny day, Dean and JoJo swam beyond the shallow reef. The water was very clear and more than a thousand feet (305 m) deep. Dean looked around for JoJo. But JoJo wasn't paying attention. He was busy sending out sonar clicks. Then he disappeared! Dean was about to head back

Humpback whales love to sing. Their songs sometimes last for hours. Scientists think they are talking to other whales or trying to attract mates with their singing.

to the reef when he heard chirping. He turned around. JoJo had brought a giant treasure to share with Dean. It was the size of a small whale. Actually, it *was* a whale. JoJo was guiding a baby humpback whale toward Dean!

For a few minutes, Dean swam around the whale. He'd never been this close to one before. What a wonderful present— except for one thing. Within minutes, the baby's mother appeared. She was a full-grown whale. Dean thought she was about 60 feet (18.3 m) long. She probably weighed 50,000 pounds (22,680 kg) or more. And she was not happy.

Dolphins vs. Sharks

Dolphins and sharks both live in the water. But they don't have a lot in common. Dolphins are mammals. They have lungs and breathe air. Their bodies are covered in skin. Dolphins swim by moving their tails up and down. Sharks are fish. They are covered in scales. They take air out of the water through their gills. Sharks swim by moving their tails from side to side.

Mother humpback whales keep their babies close to them for at least a year. They swim so close that they often touch each other.

This mother whale wanted her calf to swim away from Dean and back to her. She swam circles around Dean and the baby to get the baby's attention. Like all humpback whales, she was powerful. Her swimming created a whirlpool. Dean's heart started to pound. He was afraid he would get sucked into the swirling water. But just then, the whale stopped. She swam underneath Dean and rested. The calf joined her. They made noises at each other, like they were talking. Perhaps she was scolding her baby for leaving her. Then she rolled onto her back.

And with one eye, she looked right into Dean's eyes. It might have been a warning, but Dean didn't think so. He thought it was just two mammals making a connection. Then, with a wave of her tail, the mother whale swam off with her baby.

Dean and JoJo have had many adventures. They've even been in movies together. One movie filmed them swimming with each other. Dean had become almost as good a swimmer as JoJo. He and JoJo did barrel rolls over each other. They spun around each other. They were like underwater ballet dancers.

Another time they were asked to be in a movie about free diving. Free diving is a sport in which people hold their breath underwater. They swim along a cable to go as deep as they can. JoJo saw the cameras. He swam up to them. He could see himself in the lenses. Like most dolphins, he was fascinated. He kept looking at himself. He turned his face this way and that.

Dean thought he heard the crew up above yelling. He looked around to see a hammerhead shark swimming straight toward him! He turned and bumped into JoJo. JoJo was trying to put himself between Dean and the shark. He wasn't going to let anything hurt his friend. The shark angled down. Its rough, scaly skin scraped Dean's knee. JoJo threw himself in between the shark and Dean. He pushed the shark deeper into the water. Then he smacked the shark with his rostrum. He had to do it a few times. Finally, he chased the shark away!

Dean and JoJo have been friends for years. They've built up a strong trust.

As JoJo got older, he became interested in female dolphins. He would bring his latest girlfriend to meet Dean. Dolphins don't usually mate for life. A male dolphin can have calves with several different females. Young males leave their mothers. They join their own pods. But most females stay near their mothers all their lives. JoJo now has five children. Dean thinks that he has mated several times with the same female. Dean calls this dolphin Chenoa (sounds like cheh-NOH-uh). She is very close to one calf. Dean calls him MoJo.

As a father, JoJo spends time with his children. So he and Dean don't see each other as often as they used to. And Dean spends time traveling around the world. He is working to help humans understand cetaceans. He tells his stories about JoJo. Dean helps humans realize how smart dolphins are. He says that JoJo is an ambassador (sounds like am-BASS-uh-der) for his species (sounds like SPEE-sheez).

Dean works hard to keep dolphins safe. But he still visits the islands every couple of months. When he arrives, the first thing he does is look for his friend. When JoJo sees him, he gets very excited.

"He's like a kid getting to open a present," says Dean. And Dean probably acts the same way. Because that's what best friends do.

DOLPHINS TAKE CHARGE: FLIP NICKLIN, Photographer

Flip photographs the "auntie" dolphin.

Romeo the dolphin

Chapter 1

REVOLVING ROMEO

Meet Charles Nicklin. You can call him "Flip." Most people think he got this nickname because of his job. He's an underwater photographer. He wears flippers when he dives. But his nickname has nothing to do with swimming. Flip's father used to read a comic book called *Terry and the Pirates*. One of the characters was named Flip Corkin.

Flip Nicklin has spent his life taking pictures of underwater animals like dolphins and whales. It hasn't always been easy. He has had his share of adventures. Flip was born into an "underwater" family. Some might say he was part cetacean (sounds like sih-TAY-shun).

Flip's grandfather on his mother's side was a diver. He didn't have fancy diving gear. He just wore a hard hat underwater. Flip's dad, Chuck Nicklin, was a diver, too. He taught Flip to dive when Flip was 11 years old. Flip took to it like a duck to water. By the time Flip was 14, he was teaching others how to dive, too.

One day Flip's dad saw a wild Bryde's (sounds like BROO-dess) whale. Bryde's whales live all year long in the warm waters by the Equator. This one was floating in place. His dad thought that was strange. He swam closer. Then he figured out that the whale was tangled up in a net. Flip's father called some friends over. He climbed onto the whale's back. He and the others untangled the whale's tail. Then he slid off the whale's back. But just before he did, someone snapped a picture. It looked like Flip's dad was riding the whale! The photo was published in a magazine article.

Flip didn't know it then, but that photograph would steer his life. A lot of people saw the photograph.

A World of Dolphins

Dolphins live all over the world. Most live in the salty ocean. Some live in freshwater rivers. Most dolphins choose warm water. A few, like the orca, prefer the chillier waters near the poles. Some dolphins are picky. They like to stay in one area. Hector's dolphins swim in shallow water near the shore. No one knows why, but they are only found in the shallow water off the coast of New Zealand. The Maui (sounds like MOUW-ee) dolphin is a type of Hector's dolphin. It's the smallest of all dolphins—only four feet (1.2 m) long!

One person who saw the picture was a famous photographer. He was also a diver. He wanted Flip's dad to teach him more about whales. Soon, other people were coming to Flip's father to ask about whales and for diving lessons. Flip's dad asked Flip to help with the lessons. Before long, they were teaching photographers from around the world. Flip got interested in their work. He wanted to learn about taking pictures underwater.

In no time, he had opportunities. Flip got a job working on a film about whales. He volunteered with some researchers he met. Then he was hired to help a National Geographic explorer. What luck! He could learn more about whales and practice some photography, too. Two of the pictures he took during the dives were published in the article. After that, he went to a lot of places to take pictures. He even spent time near the Arctic Circle. *Brrr!* The water was pretty chilly there. He had to wear a dry suit. It's a waterproof suit that divers wear to keep warm. But Flip didn't always work in cold places. And he didn't only photograph whales.

Once, he was asked to take pictures of dolphins. Some scientists were studying Atlantic spotted dolphins. They live in the Atlantic Ocean. Many live near the Bahamas. The water there is warm. It would be a nice change from the cold!

Atlantic spotted dolphins have long bodies. They are usually 7.5 feet (2.3 m) long. Their skin is dark gray on the top and white underneath. They are born without spots. Like Dalmatian dogs, their spots appear as they get older. They have all their spots by the time they are 15 years old. No two animals have the same pattern of spots. That makes it easier for scientists to identify specific dolphins.

Dolphins are smaller than most other whales. But they can swim fast. They can easily outswim even the fastest human swimmers, like Olympian Michael Phelps. Keeping up with a dolphin can make a photographer's job hard. Most photographers spend time setting up a shot. Flip soon learned that wasn't how it worked with dolphins. When it comes to photos, dolphins are in charge.

Flip and the researchers took a small boat out looking for the dolphins. They anchored the boat and waited for wild dolphins to come by. *There!* They spied a group. Quickly, Flip put on his fins and mask. He grabbed his camera and swung his legs over the side of the boat and slipped into the water.

Within moments, a dolphin came speeding up. Then he stopped, like a car braking for a red light. Dolphins are curious about a lot of things. This one stared right into Flip's camera. Then he slowly swam around Flip. Flip turned

Did You Know?

Dolphins can swim faster than 20 miles an hour (32 km/h). That's as fast as a car!

to keep the dolphin in his sight. The dolphin swam a little faster. So Flip swam a little faster. Then that little rascal swam even faster. Flip did, too. Before long, Flip was spinning like a top. He was totally dizzy. Flip had to stop. That playful dolphin gave a flip of his fluke and swam off to play with someone else. When Flip told the scientists what had happened, they nearly fell over laughing.

They told him that the dolphin he had met was Romeo (sounds like ROH-mee-o). Romeo was a trickster. He loved to play the spinning game with people. It was his special trick. And like many others, Flip had fallen for it.

Flip Nicklin uses a special underwater camera to capture images of dolphins and other ocean life.

Chapter 2

Romeo had taught Flip a lesson—dolphins love to play! That was good to know. He would be prepared the next time he took dolphin pictures. And as it turned out, he would use that lesson in a special way. Another group of scientists was studying dolphins. Some time ago, dolphin populations were dying off. The scientists needed to find out why.

And soon they did. The problem was fishing nets. Fishermen used rope nets to catch tuna and other fish for people to eat. They often fished in areas where dolphins fished. It seems that dolphins and people like to eat a lot of the same kinds of fish. And dolphins are very good at finding them. So when the fishermen saw dolphins, they threw their nets into the water. The large rope nets caught lots of fish.

But the nets also caught the dolphins. The dolphins became tangled and then trapped in the nets. Dolphins aren't fish. They are mammals. They need to breathe air every 15 minutes. The nets kept them from reaching the surface of the water.

Thousands of dolphins were drowning in fishermen's nets. The scientists wanted to write an article to tell people about this problem. Although Flip usually took pictures of whales, they asked him to help with the article by taking dolphin photos.

Flip agreed. Soon he was traveling around the world taking pictures of dolphins for the story. At one point, he was in Hawaii (sounds like huh-WHY-ee), U.S.A. Hawaii is made up of several islands.

The capital of Hawaii is on the island of Oahu (sounds like oh-AH-hoo). But the biggest island is named Hawaii. Biologists (sounds like by-AH-loh-jists) were studying dolphins there. They had built a large pool for the dolphins to swim in. It was called a lagoon (sounds like luh-GOON). Tourists were allowed in the lagoon, too. They could swim with the dolphins.

To take clear pictures, Flip needed the water to be as still as possible. So he woke up really early one morning. He wanted to be in the water before anyone else.

To photograph whales and dolphins, Flip used a special waterproof box for his camera. It looked like a large, glowing eye. *Do the dolphins think I'm a giant squid?* he sometimes wondered. He sealed the camera into its waterproof case. He put on his fins. He slipped into the lagoon. He counted as many dolphins as he could see swimming around. He thought he saw 11.

Band of Dolphins

Dolphins band together to help each other. Sometimes it's to hunt. They swim in a circle or a horseshoe (HOR-shoo) to herd fish for a meal. They join up for other reasons, too. One scientist saw dolphins swim right next to each other. Then they started to move their tails together, like synchronized (sounds like SING-kruh-nized) swimmers. They copied each other's sounds. She wondered what they were doing. Then she figured it out. They were trying to make themselves look bigger and stronger and sound louder. That way, they could scare away large sharks.

Flip ducked
underwater so
the dolphins
could get a good
look at him and get
used to him. Soon, some
of the dolphins came up to him.

One dolphin had a baby with her.
Baby dolphins are called calves.
Calves usually stay with their mothers
until they are at least a year and a half old.
Their mothers have a lot to teach them.
Flip once saw an orca teaching her baby
to fish. She chased a salmon until it was
close enough for the baby to catch.
Gulp! The baby had a tasty meal.

This dolphin's calf was young. Flip
wanted to get pictures of it with its mother.

But he knew that mothers can be protective of their babies. Luckily, she didn't seem to mind him. Flip swam around them, trying to get a good shot. Suddenly, another female came sailing toward him. She bumped Flip with her snout, or rostrum. She tried to shove him away. It took him a minute to understand. She was protecting the baby.

Biologists think that some female dolphins help take care of other dolphins' calves. Sometimes it's a dolphin related to the new mother, like a sister or an aunt.

Did You Know?

When Flip started diving, he was too young to scuba. So he started with free diving. Free diving means diving without an air mask. It takes a lot of practice. But Flip can hold his breath for several minutes. He can dive as deep as 90 feet (27 m).

These "auntie" dolphins babysit while the mother looks for food. They can also help fight off sharks. Flip was pretty sure he had met an auntie.

After a number of tries, Flip had to give up. Auntie just wouldn't let him get close. He swam away. He floated on the bottom of the pool. Before long, the mother and her calf came up to him. Like most dolphins, they were curious. But it didn't last. *Wham!* Auntie was back, too. She thrust herself in between Flip and the baby.

The lagoon had a sandy bottom. Flip ran his hand along the sand. He felt something at his fingertips. *What's that?*

Did You Know?

Baby dolphins can be 33 inches (84 cm) to 55 inches (140 cm) long. That means a newborn dolphin is about as long as a guitar.

It was a leaf on a twig. That's when he remembered Romeo. Romeo had played a game with him. *Maybe I can play one with Auntie,* Flip thought. Flip dropped the twig slowly. Auntie grabbed it and tossed it back. *Game on!*

Flip kept picking the twig up with one hand and clicking the camera with the other. But he became distracted. He grabbed for the leaf too quickly.

Chomp! Auntie clamped her mouth down on his hand. She let go quickly, but not before leaving tooth marks. Flip didn't mind too much. Believe it or not, he had taken some great pictures.

Misha is gently guided back into the wild.

Chapter 3

THE RETURN OF ECHO AND MISHA

Through his work, Flip had met Dr. Randy Wells. Randy had loved dolphins since he was a kid. He became a biologist. Randy worked with dolphins in Tampa Bay, Florida, U.S.A. Randy's boss wanted to learn more about dolphin sounds. He put together a team of scientists and built a special lab. Now he needed two wild dolphins.

Flip was interested in Randy's work. So he joined the team to take pictures. The team caught two dolphins in Tampa Bay. They named them Echo and Misha. They put the dolphins on a plane in special water-filled containers.

Randy and the rest of the team flew with them to the lab in California, U.S.A. They didn't plan to keep the dolphins forever. They just wanted to work with and study the dolphins for two years. Then they would take the dolphins back to Florida.

When the dolphins were returned to Florida, the scientists would conduct a second experiment. They would return the dolphins to the wild. They would keep checking on the dolphins for one year. They were hoping they could find out something important: Could dolphins be taken care of by people and then return to the wild?

The team worked with the dolphins and learned new things about echolocation (sounds like ek-oh-loh-KAY- shun). The two years flew by. Soon it was time to take the dolphins home. They took the dolphins back to Florida but didn't release them right away.

The dolphins stayed in a sea pen at a lab near Sarasota (sounds like sar-uh-SOH-tuh). The dolphins needed to get used to the bay water again. The team fed them local fish. They made sure the dolphins were healthy. After three and a half weeks, Echo and Misha were ready to return to the spot where they had been caught.

You Can Help

Today, fishermen must use dolphin-safe
nets. But dolphins face other dangers.
Boat propellers can hurt them. And the
noise from boats makes it hard for them
to use echolocation to find food. Pollution
from factories near the water can poison
their food. Then the dolphins become
sick. You can help. Try to recycle what
you use. That keeps water pollution
down. Try not to use chemicals that can
end up in the ocean. And always leave the
beach clean after a day in the sun!

This was a big event. Most people were excited about the release. But some were worried. What if the dolphins had forgotten how to live on their own? Echo and Misha were young males. Young male dolphins often become best buddies, and they had. This might help them when they returned to the wild.

On the day of the release, the area was crowded with reporters, scientists, and photographers. Flip was there, too. He had been there when the dolphins were caught. He didn't want to miss this important moment in their story.

Flip motored out in a separate boat. His little boat was pretty far away from the boat that held the dolphins. He would have to move fast when Echo and Misha went into the water. Some team members were already in the water. Flip waited on the boat until the team gave the signal. The animals were gently lowered into the water in slings. He jumped in, too.

Flip swam closer to be near Echo and Misha. Members of the team held the dolphins. They pointed them toward the deep water. On Randy's signal, they let go. Echo and Misha dipped down a little, then popped their heads up for air. Flip was ready. *Click, click, click.*

The dolphins glided to a shallow area where the water was less than three feet (1 m) deep. Then they just floated there, making clicking sounds. Flip waited again.

Are they okay? he wondered. Then Flip remembered that dolphins have very good hearing. And they have their own superpower—echolocation. Were they sending out clicks to find out who or what was near? Did they hear other animals close by? Time passed. It seemed like forever to him. He started to worry. Maybe the dolphins couldn't live in the wild again.

As Flip watched, the team gently guided the dolphins back to deeper water. Again the dolphins flippered to shallow water. They moved their heads back and forth. Randy and the head trainer tried one more time. This time, they swam alongside the dolphins.

Suddenly, without any warning, Echo and Misha flipped their tails and swam off. Luckily, Flip was ready. He snapped a picture of them just as they swam away!

Flip learned later that there was a group of dolphins nearby. Echo and Misha must have known where they were. When they were ready, they swam off to join them.

Members of the team often checked up on Echo and Misha. After a few weeks, the dolphins went their separate ways. But both were healthy and living with other dolphins. They had been able to return to the wild!

Both Echo and Misha were seen many times in Tampa Bay. Twenty-five years later, Echo had been spotted more than 60 times.

Over the years, Flip has made thousands of dives and taken many photographs. His pictures help others understand these wonderful creatures that share our world.

THE END

DON'T MISS!

NATIONAL GEOGRAPHIC KiDS **CHAPTERS**

HERO DOGS!

True Stories
of Amazing
Animal
Heroes!

F 10

Mary Quattlebaum

**Turn the page
for a sneak preview . . .**

Molly, Coco, and a special friend

MOLLY and COCO: CONSERVATION CHAMPS!

Molly and Coco greet their new friend.

Chapter 1

WELCOME HOME!

Molly and Coco trotted beside Anna Tolan in the big house in Africa. A new animal had arrived, and they wanted to meet him. The Jack Russell terriers loved welcoming wild animals to their home, the Chipembele (sounds like CHIP-em-beh-leh) Wildlife Education Trust, in Mfuwe, Zambia (sounds like Mm-FOO-ee, ZAM-bee-uh).

Molly and Coco greeted everyone who came, from small squirrels to large elephants. Anna and her husband, Steve, opened the door. Molly and Coco dashed outside. They raced over the dirt to a big covered pen called a boma (sounds like BO-mah). Something was moving inside!

Anna opened the gate. And there stood a baby hippopotamus! The dogs raced straight for the calf, then they jumped on him. *Lick, lick, lick.* They licked and licked his gray skin.

Douglas, the hippo, stayed very still. He didn't try to run. He didn't chase the dogs. Those licks felt good!

Molly and Coco continued to lick. *Welcome to Chipembele,* they seemed to say. *You are safe here, Douglas. We are friendly.*

Licking is how the dogs greet most newcomers, said Anna. That's how they say hello. The licking often calms the frightened animals, too. Most of the animals that come to Chipembele are motherless. Some are hurt. They are brought to the wildlife sanctuary (sounds like SANK-choo-air-ee) for care and medical treatment. The licking helps to relax them. If an animal is calm, it often eats better and heals more quickly.

There was a lot of Douglas to lick! This big baby weighed 111 pounds (50 kg). His size didn't stop the dogs, though. They

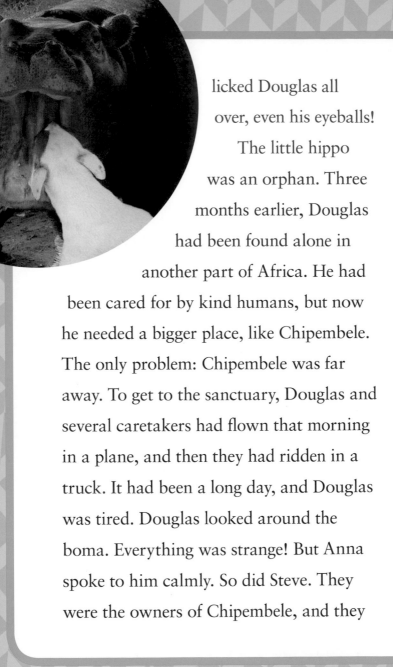

licked Douglas all over, even his eyeballs! The little hippo was an orphan. Three months earlier, Douglas had been found alone in another part of Africa. He had been cared for by kind humans, but now he needed a bigger place, like Chipembele. The only problem: Chipembele was far away. To get to the sanctuary, Douglas and several caretakers had flown that morning in a plane, and then they had ridden in a truck. It had been a long day, and Douglas was tired. Douglas looked around the boma. Everything was strange! But Anna spoke to him calmly. So did Steve. They were the owners of Chipembele, and they made sure all the animals were safe and cared for. Molly and Coco gave Douglas a few more licks. The hippo relaxed. He drank some milk and went to sleep.

But soon he was awake again and hungry! Hippo calves eat a lot. For the next several days, three keepers cared for Douglas constantly. They fed him every three hours, day and night. Anna, Molly, and Coco checked on him often.

The dogs loved to visit their new friend. They especially liked what happened after he drank his milk. Douglas would open his huge mouth. The two dogs would put their heads inside. Douglas would hold very still. Then the dogs would lick up any last drops of milk. Molly and Coco had a little snack, thanks to Douglas.

The Power of Touch

Babies need more than food to survive. Many animal babies need to be held, touched, and groomed. This helps their brains and bodies to develop. Scientists have learned this by studying monkeys and rats. Animal babies that were not touched grew more slowly. They were nervous and depressed. When they became mothers, they did not care for their own babies very well. Touch continues to be important as children and animals grow into adulthood. It helps to lessen stress and worry. Have you ever gotten a hug from a friend when you were having a bad day or when you were sad? Did you feel better? That's the power of touch!

Douglas loved the attention and licks from the dogs. Their tongues probably felt a little like his mother's tongue. To grow big and healthy, many young animals need more than food. They also need to be stroked and groomed. They need to be cleaned and cuddled. In the wild, they usually receive this care from their mothers. But orphans like Douglas might get it from other animals or humans.

Some heroes do big, brave acts. Some, like Molly and Coco, are heroes by doing what they do every day at Chipembele. They help to care for baby animals that could not survive on their own. Over the years, the dogs have assisted with . . .

Want to know what happens next? Be sure to check out *Hero Dogs!* Available wherever books and ebooks are sold.

INDEX

Boldface indicates illustrations.

Amazon River dolphins 77
Aquariums 8, 33
Atlantic spotted dolphins 76–77

Baleen whales 9
Boat propellers 53, 94
Body language 47
Bryde's whales 72–73, **73**

Cetaceans 9, 52, 67, 72

Dolphin shows 8, 12, 33, **33**
Dolphins
    babies **86,** 86–88, **89**
    blowholes 11, 54
    dogs as friends 55, **55**
    echolocation 19, 23, 25, 93,
        94, 97
    how to help 94
    intelligence 7, 8, 12, 19, 23–25
    jumping **5,** 40
    language 44, 47
    play **6,** 11, 59, 79, 81, 83
    solitary dolphins 55
    tool use 15

ELVIS project 23

Fishing nets 73, 82–83, 94
Free diving 64–65, 87

Hector's dolphins 74, **74**
Humpback whales 61, 63
Hurricane Katrina (2005) 26,
    27–30

Institute for Marine Mammal
    Studies (IMMS), Gulfport,
    Mississippi, U.S.A. 10–11,
    26, 28, 29, 30

Mammals 8, 62, 82
Maui dolphins 74
Mirrors 22, **22**

National Aquarium, Baltimore,
    Maryland, U.S.A. 33

Oceanariums 8, 52
Orcas 8, 35, 74, 86

Pointing 47
Pollution 94
Porpoises 9, 13, **13**

Recycling 94

Sea lions 30, 31
Seaweed 11, 83
Sharks 46, 62, **62,** 65, 85,
    88, 96

Toothed whales 9, 13